PUNCH *parties*

PUNCH *parties*

Punches, pitchers, and refreshing cocktails
to share with friends

Ben Reed

photography by

William Lingwood

RYLAND
PETERS
& SMALL

LONDON NEW YORK

Senior Designer Barbara Zuñiga
Editor Rebecca Woods
Picture Research Emily Westlake
Production Gordana Simakovic
Art Director Leslie Harrington
Editorial Director Julia Charles

Indexer Hilary Bird
Prop Stylist Lucy Harvey
Drink Stylist Ben Reed
Food Stylist Lucy Mckelvie

First published in 2012
by Ryland Peters & Small
20–21 Jockey's Fields
London WC1R 4BW
and
519 Broadway, 5th Floor
New York, NY 10012

www.rylandpeters.com

10 9 8 7 6 5 4 3 2 1

Text © Ben Reed 2012
with the exception of the food recipes on pages 104–121
© Ghillie Basan, Jules Beresford, Ross Dobson, and
Lydia France
Design and commissioned photographs
© Ryland Peters & Small 2012

ISBN 978 1 84975 206 0

US Library of Congress cataloging-in-publication data
has been applied for.

A catalogue record for this book is available from the
British Library.

Printed in China

Notes
- Measurements are occasionally given in barspoons,
  which are equivalent to 5 ml or one teaspoon.
- All ice refers to ice cubes, unless otherwise stated.
- When using the zest of citrus fruits, try to find organic
  or unwaxed fruits and wash well before using. If you can
  only find treated fruit, scrub well with warm soapy water
  and rinse before using.

Contents

Introduction

Punches are enduring in their popularity, and make a perfect party drink, fashionable all over the world. They are actually considered to be the world's first global cocktail. Originating in India in the 17th century, the concept made its way back to the UK and then through Europe and the rest of the world through the trade links of the British East India Company.

There are differing insights into the origins of the word "punch"; some say it comes from the Hindustani word *panch*, others that it comes from the Persian *panj*, both meaning five, as punch was originally a drink containing five ingredients: spirit, sugar, citrus, spice, and water. Other historians suggest that the expression derived from the word *puncheon*, a large wooden cask that could be converted into a vessel that would hold a large amount of liquid from which the drink was served. These days anything served in a large bowl is generally referred to as punch. They are perfect at parties as they can be prepared in advance and thirsty guests can gratefully help themselves.

There is a punch for every occasion, any level of enthusiasm, all seasons, and containing as many variations of spirit as one could imagine; contrary to popular belief, punches do not have to be made solely from rum. Nor do they have to be served from a single bowl—many classic punches have their own serving vessels specifically designed to match the drink, whether it's a fun Tiki mug or sophisticated coupette glass.

What actually classifies a drink as a punch is the proportions of the ingredients you use. The traditional rhyme which will help you remember how to balance your 4 main ingredients is: "Use one (part) of sour, two of sweet, three of strong, and four of weak." Here the "sour" was traditionally lime or lemon juice, the "sweet" a sweetener such as agave syrup, the "strong" is the spirit, and the "weak" a diluting ingredient such as water or fruit juice.

If you do choose to serve punch from a bowl (or a pitcher), remember that bulk preparation of a cocktail doesn't mean you should cut corners! Use good quality alcohol and where juice is included try to use freshly squeezed or, at the very least, avoid anything made from concentrate.

Don't skimp on the garnishes, they're not just there to make the drink look good. A fresh sprig of mint added to a cocktail lends it's bearer a zippy freshness. The zests of citrus fruit play an important role too; when zesting try not to peel away any of the bitter white pith.

Large blocks of ice are perfect for punch bowls as they will dilute at a much slower rate than smaller cubes, perfect if the punch will be sitting

in the bowl for a time. To make large blocks of ice, simply add still mineral water to a plastic container and leave in the freezer overnight. If you are making blended drinks using ice, always make sure to crush the ice cubes first by putting them in a freezer bag and pounding with a rolling pin—this will preserve the blades of your blender.

And finally to your serving equipment. The punch bowl can be made from china, cut glass, or sterling silver—it doesn't really matter so long as it has the capacity to hold liquid and look attractive. Your punch bowl should be the centerpiece for the night's festivities and you are using it so that you're not stuck in the kitchen all night making drinks, so try to find one that one that will contain enough liquid for a least two servings per guest. Although many bowls come with matching cups, you can also be creative, serving punch in glasses, tea cups, or even small bowls.

If you are serving the single drinks, suggestions have been provided in the recipe for the type of glasses these punches were originally served in. Here, each recipe makes 1 drink, so you can easily scale up the quantities to cater for as many guests as you have.

And finally, don't forget a piece of equipment that is often overlooked and whose absence can quite often lead to a sticky mess; the ladle.

Party Punches

These refreshing, sophisticated punches are perfect for serving on occasions when you are entertaining a thirsty crowd. Serve in large punch bowls with a ladle so guests can gleefully help themselves.

Tom Collins

Although many consider the Tom Collins to be an English drink, this early punch was actually first documented by Professor Jerry Thomas, the father of American cocktails, in the 2nd edition of *The Bartender's Guide* in 1876, and has remained a cocktail-party classic ever since.

2 cups / 500 ml London dry gin
1 cup / 250 ml fresh lemon juice
   (about 6 lemons)
½ cup / 125 ml fresh fruit purée
   (pomegranate, raspberry, and
   blueberry purées are all good)
½ cup / 125 ml sugar syrup
   (see note, right)
4 cups / 1 litre soda water, to top up
seasonal fresh fruit, to garnish

Serves 10

Add all the ingredients except the soda water to a pitcher or punch bowl filled with ice and stir gently to mix. Top up with soda water and stir again.

Serve in tall ice-filled glasses, garnished with seasonal fresh fruit.

Note: To make a basic sugar syrup, put 2 cups/400 g superfine/caster sugar and 1 cup/250 ml water in a saucepan set over low heat. Heat gently, stirring frequently, until the sugar has dissolved. Remove from the heat and leave to cool.

Singapore Sling

Created at the Long Bar at the Raffles hotel in Singapore, when this drink is made correctly, and without using one of the cheap pre-mixes that are so prevalent today, it is the peak of sophistication! The original recipe has long been a subject of hot debate, but this is the one I favor.

2 cups / 500 ml gin
¾ cup / 200 ml cherry brandy
⅓ cup / 100 ml Benedictine
¾ cup / 200 ml fresh lemon juice
   (about 5 lemons)
1 teaspoon Angostura bitters
soda water, to top up
lemon zest curls and cocktail
   cherries, to garnish

Serves 10

Put all the ingredients in a pitcher or punch bowl filled with ice and stir gently to mix. Top up with soda water.

Serve in tall, ice-filled glasses, garnished with a lemon zest curl and a cocktail cherry.

ON GARNISHING

Garnishes are an essential element of punch. This one can be easily assembled by taking a long thin piece of lemon zest, rolling it around a cocktail cherry, and holding it in place with a toothpick.

Fish House Punch

This is the official punch of the oldest club in America, the Schuylkill Fishing Company. Its strength was and is legendary, perhaps in an attempt to liven up a long morning angling. If you want to bring down the strength, let it sit on the ice for a while to dilute it a little.

1 cup/250 ml fresh lemon juice
(about 6 lemons)
½ cup/100 g superfine/caster sugar
2 cups/500 ml dark Jamaican rum
1 cup/250 ml Cognac
generous oz./30 ml peach brandy
2 cups/500 ml mineral water
(still or sparkling)
pared lemon zest, to garnish

Serves 10

Put the lemon juice and sugar in a large punch bowl and stir until the sugar is dissolved.

Add the remaining ingredients to the bowl along with a large block of ice, and stir gently to mix. Garnish with strips of lemon zest and serve in punch cups or glasses.

Mai Tai

The Mai Tai is the flagship cocktail of the Tiki movement—a
Polynesian theme that began in the 1930s and is going strong today.
You will see this drink made a hundred different ways in bars around
the world, but this is Trader Vic's original recipe.

2 cups/500 ml dark Jamaican rum
1¼ cups/300 ml fresh lime juice
   (about 10 limes)
⅔ cup/150 ml orange curaçao
⅔ cup/150 ml orgeat syrup
scant ¼ cup/50 ml sugar syrup
   (see page 10)
pineapple slices and fresh mint sprigs,
   to garnish

Serves 10

Pour all the ingredients into a large punch bowl filled with ice and stir
gently to mix.

Serve in ice-filled Tiki mugs (if you have them) or glasses, garnished
with pineapple slices and mint sprigs.

Regent's Punch

Also known as the George IV punch, it is often thought that the tea in this punch was the only thing that kept the Prince Regent on his feet! With the addition of Champagne, it makes a great party punch for a special occasion, served from a classic bowl into dainty cups.

2⅓ cups / 600 ml Earl Grey tea
pared zest of 3 lemons
pared zest of 1 orange
1 cup / 200 g superfine / caster sugar
1 cup / 250 ml Cognac
⅔ cup / 150 ml dark Jamaican rum
1 cup / 250 ml fresh lemon juice
   (about 6 lemons)
1 cup / 250 ml pineapple juice
1 x 75-cl bottle Champagne

Serves 10

Make up the Earl Grey tea and add the lemon and orange zests and sugar whilst still hot. Stir and set aside to cool.

When cooled, add to a large punch bowl with the Cognac, rum, and lemon and pineapple juices. Stir gently to mix and add a large block of ice. Top up with the Champagne just before serving in punch cups or glasses.

Maui Punch

Captain Cook first discovered the pineapple in Hawaii in 1778, though it was first introduced there by the Polynesians. Very soon it was a staple in punch bowls across America. It lends a hint of the exotic and tropical, as well as a soft caramel sweetness that works with most spirits.

4 pineapples, peeled, cored, and sliced
1 lb./450 g superfine/caster sugar
1 cup/250 ml dark Jamaican rum
1 cup/250 ml Cognac
⅔ cup/150 ml orange curaçao
⅔ cup/150 ml fresh lemon juice
   (about 4 lemons)
4 x 75-cl bottles Champagne

Serves 10

Put the pineapple slices in a large punch bowl. Sprinkle over the sugar and leave to stand, overnight if possible, until the sugar has soaked into the pineapple slices.

After this time, add the rum, Cognac, curaçao, lemon juice, and Champagne to the punch bowl along with a block of ice. Stir gently to mix and serve in punch cups or glasses.

Kentucky Cooler

We all know that Bourbon works beautifully with mint in the Julep. This
is a longer, more refreshing version, lengthened with grapefruit, soda, and
a dash of bitters. Just add ice, a veranda, and some sun, and enjoy!

2⅓ cups/600 ml Bourbon whiskey
4 cups/1 litre fresh pink grapefruit
    juice (about 10 grapefruits)
1 teaspoon Angostura bitters
1 cup/250 ml soda water
10 fresh mint sprigs, to garnish

mint-infused syrup
1 cup/200 g superfine/caster sugar
5 fresh mint sprigs

Serves 10

To make the mint sugar syrup, put the sugar, mint, and ½ cup/125 ml
water in a saucepan set over low heat. Heat gently, stirring frequently,
until the sugar has dissolved. Remove from the heat and leave to cool,
then strain out the mint.

Add the mint syrup to a pitcher or punch bowl with the whiskey,
grapefruit juice, and Angostura bitters and stir gently to mix. Add
a block of ice and top up with the soda water just before serving.

Serve in tall, ice-filled glasses, garnished with a mint sprig.

Classic Cosmopolitan Punch

To make the perfect Cosmopolitan, you need to ensure that you balance the drink correctly. The sour (the limes) and the sweet (the Cointreau) should be measured equally to give the cocktail a sharp citrussy taste.

2 cups/500 ml lemon vodka
1 cup/250 ml fresh lime juice
    (about 8 limes)
1 cup/250 ml Cointreau
2 cups/500 ml cranberry juice
orange slices, to garnish

Serves 10

Add all the ingredients to a large punch bowl filled with ice and stir gently to mix.

Serve in punch cups or glasses garnished with orange slices.

Bitter Cosmopolitan Punch

I consider that many cocktail recipes are open to a bit of tweaking and the addition of grapefruit vodka and orange bitters adds a little more depth to this classic cocktail.

2 cups/500 ml grapefruit vodka
    (such as Finlandia)
1 scant cup/225 ml orange
    curaçao
¾ cup/200 ml fresh lime juice
    (about 6 limes)
1⅓ cups/350 ml cranberry juice
½ cup/100 ml fresh grapefruit
    juice (about 1 grapefruit)
1 teaspoon orange bitters
pared grapefruit zest, to garnish

Serves 10

Add all the ingredients to a large punch bowl filled with ice and stir gently to mix.

Serve in punch cups or glasses garnished with grapefruit zest.

Russian Spring Punch

**Created in London's Soho by legendary bartender Dick Bradsell, this
sophisticated punch has all the elements of a perfect summer tipple:
fresh berries, tangy lemon juice, and cool, refreshing bubbles.**

2 cups / 500 ml premium vodka
⅔ cup / 150 ml crème de cassis
1⅓ cups / 350 ml fresh lemon juice
  (about 9 lemons)
⅔ cup / 150 ml sugar syrup
  (see page 10)
Champagne, to top up
raspberries, lemon husks, and fresh
  mint sprigs, to garnish

Serves 10

Add the vodka, crème de cassis, lemon juice, and sugar syrup to a large
punch bowl filled with ice and stir gently to mix.

Top up with the Champagne just before serving and stir again. Garnish
with raspberries, lemon husks, and mint sprigs and serve in punch
cups or glasses.

Pisco Punch

This delightful punch is made using the lesser-known spirit Pisco,
a Peruvian grape brandy made from the Muscat grape. It's a variation
on the Pisco Sour—made with lemon, sugar, and bitters—which
I consider to be much improved with the addition of pineapple.

1 x 70 cl bottle Pisco brandy
1⅓ cups / 350 ml fresh lemon juice
   (about 9 lemons)
2 cups / 500 ml mineral water
   (still or sparkling)

pineapple-infused syrup
1 small pineapple, peeled, cored,
   and sliced
2½ cups / 500 g superfine / caster
   sugar

Serves 10

To make the pineapple syrup, put the sugar and 1¼ cups / 300 ml water
in a saucepan set over low heat. Heat gently, stirring frequently, until the
sugar has dissolved. Remove from the heat and leave to cool a little. Add
the pineapple slices and let them infuse in the syrup for a few hours, or
overnight if possible. Before using the syrup, remove the pineapple slices
and reserve them for the garnish.

Add the pineapple syrup and the other punch ingredients to a pitcher
or punch bowl filled with ice and stir gently to mix.

Serve in ice-filled glasses garnished with the reserved pineapple slices.

Pomegranate Punch

Babicka is a truly unique Czech vodka that is infused with wormwood (the key ingredient of absinthe) and which works curiously well with pomegranate. If you can't find Babicka, you can substitute your favorite vodka, flavored or otherwise.

2 cups / 500 ml Babicka vodka
3 cups / 750 ml pomegranate juice
2 cups / 500 ml fresh grapefruit juice
   (about 5 grapefruits)
1 cup / 250 ml fresh lime juice
   (about 8 limes)
⅔ cup / 150 ml sugar syrup
   (see page 10)
2 cups / 500 ml soda water, to serve
pared grapefruit zest and fresh mint
   sprigs, to garnish

Put the vodka, the pomegranate, grapefruit, and lime juices, and the sugar syrup in a large punch bowl or pitcher filled with ice. Top up with soda water, and stir gently to mix.

Serve in ice-filled highball glasses, garnished with a grapefruit zest spiral and sprigs of mint.

Serves 10

Perfect Pitchers

Pitchers are perfect when you are hosting a summer party. Circulating whilst topping up glasses from an iced pitcher is a perfect way to mingle and chat with your appreciative guests.

Mojito

The Mojito is arguably the world's most popular drink of the last
10 years and is sure to be happily received by guests. Ernest Hemingway
claimed that he drank his at La Bodeguita del Medio in Havana, a bar
still standing today.

2 cups / 500 ml light Puerto
  Rican-style rum
¾ cup / 200 ml fresh lime juice
  (about 6 limes)
⅓ cup / 100 ml sugar syrup
  (see page 10)
40 large fresh mint leaves, plus mint
  sprigs, to garnish
soda water, to top up (optional)

Serves 10

Put the rum, lime juice, sugar syrup, and mint
leaves in a pitcher filled with ice and
stir gently to mix. Top up with
soda water, if desired.

Serve in glasses filled with
crushed ice and garnish
each with a mint sprig.

MINTY FRESH

The mint garnish is so
important with this drink. Use
a healthy bushel of mint and
not only will your drink look
great but the fragrant aroma
will waft up into your nose
as you taste the
cocktail.

Kentucky Mule

A variation on the Moscow mule, this twist is a favorite of mine
as the base spirit, Bourbon, offers a little bit more flavor than the
traditional vodka and combines beautifully with the heavier flavors
of ginger beer and aromatic Angostura bitters.

1¼ cups / 300 ml Bourbon whiskey
4 cups / 1 litre spicy ginger beer
6 dashes Angostura bitters
3 limes, each cut into 8 wedges

Serves 6

Put the whiskey, ginger beer, and Angostura bitters in a large pitcher
filled with ice. Squeeze the lime wedges into the pitcher and then drop
the husks in too. Stir gently before serving in ice-filled glasses.

Paloma Punch

The literal meaning of *paloma* is "dove", although why this drink is so called is a mystery! Although it may seem a lot of effort, do try, where possible, to use freshly squeezed grapefruit juice for this cocktail to achieve that perfect summer freshness.

2 cups / 500 ml reposado tequila
⅓ cup / 100 ml agave syrup
6 cups / 1.5 litres fresh grapefruit
   juice (about 15 grapefruits)
¼ cup / 60 ml fresh lime juice
   (about 2 limes)
1 cup / 250 ml soda water
salt, for the glass

Serves 10

Put the tequila, agave syrup, and grapefruit juice in a pitcher filled with ice. Squeeze the limes into the pitcher and drop the husks in too, reserving one for preparing the glasses. Top up with the soda water and stir gently to mix.

To prepare the glasses, pour some salt onto a plate. Rub the rim of the glasses with the spent lime husk. Turn each glass upside down and place it in the salt so that it coats the rim.

Fill the salt-rimmed glasses with ice, top up with punch, and serve.

Lahara Margarita

Named after the oranges grown on the island of Curaçao, the Lahara fruit is inedibly bitter—it is the zest that is used to flavor the curaçao. The addition of blue curaçao instead of the clear variety adds a touch of fun to the drink.

2½ cups / 600 ml reposado tequila
¾ cup / 200 ml blue curaçao
¾ cup / 200 ml triple sec
1⅔ cups / 400 ml fresh lime juice
  (about 13 limes)

Serves 10

Add all the ingredients to a pitcher filled with crushed ice. Stir gently to mix and serve in punch cups or glasses.

FEELING BLUE

Blue curaçao is simply orange curaçao with food coloring added to it to lend a touch of fun and frivolity to your cocktails. You can use the clear variety if you prefer.

Kingston Cooler

For this delicious cocktail, the only ingredient you may have to look a little harder to find is the orgeat, an almond flavored syrup. Do try to pick it up online, though, as it does bring a unique flavor to the drink.

2 cups / 500 ml dark Jamaican rum
⅓ cup / 100 ml Wray and Nephew
   overproof rum
1 cup / 250 ml fresh lime juice
   (about 8 limes)
⅓ cup / 100 ml orgeat syrup
2 cups / 500 ml passion fruit juice
2 cups / 500 ml pineapple juice
seasonal fresh fruit and fresh mint
   sprigs, to garnish

Add all the ingredients to a large pitcher or punch bowl filled with ice and stir gently to mix.

Serve in ice-filled glasses garnished with seasonal fruit and mint sprigs.

Serves 10

Beachcomber's Gold

This Tiki drink was originally served in an ice shell, made by pressing crushed ice into a glass until it rises up over the sides. While this looks amazing, it takes time and may not be the best way to serve a group!

¾ cup / 200 ml honey
⅔ cup / 150 ml fresh lime juice
   (about 5 limes)
1 cup / 250 ml light Cuban-style rum
1 cup / 250 ml dark Jamaican rum
2 cups / 500 ml passion fruit juice
1 teaspoon Angostura bitters
passion fruit wedges, to garnish

Put the honey and lime juice in a pitcher and stir until the honey has dissolved.

Add the remaining ingredients and some crushed ice and stir gently to mix.

Serve in ice-filled glasses garnished with wedges of passion fruit.

Serves 10

Chi Chi

When making a Chi Chi, don't get "cream of coconut" confused with "coconut cream" (which is like coconut milk but with less water), or "creamed coconut" (which is compressed coconut flesh). The one you're looking for should be sweet—Coco Lopez is a good brand to use.

2 cups / 500 ml vodka
4 cups / 1 litre unsweetened
   pineapple juice
1 cup / 250 ml cream of coconut
   (preferably Coco Lopez)
pineapple and orange slices,
   to garnish

Serves 10

Add all the ingredients to a blender with 4 scoops of crushed ice and blitz to mix.

Pour into a pitcher and serve in Tiki mugs (if you have them) garnished with fresh pineapple and orange slices.

Rose Tinted Spectacles

This drink was created in the 90s as flavored vodkas were taking the world by storm. The currant and citrus vodkas combine with the apple juice for a light, refreshing, and zingy cocktail. A couple of these and the world just seems a nicer place.

1 cup/250 ml citrus vodka
1 cup/250 ml Kurrant vodka
2 quarts/2 litres apple juice
scant ¼ cup/50 ml sugar syrup
   (see page 10)
1 teaspoon Angostura bitters
¼ cup/60 ml fresh lime juice
   (about 2 limes)
lemon or lime slices, to garnish

Serves 10

Add all the ingredients to a pitcher filled with ice and stir gently to mix.

Serve in tall ice-filled glasses, garnished with lemon or lime slices.

Ten Green Bottles

Elderflower is a wonderful cocktail flavoring and Bottle Green is one of the best brands to use. It is sold globally, or should be available online. Do experiment with the brand of pomegranate juice you use as some are more authentic than others.

1⅔ cups / 400 ml vodka
¾ cup / 200 ml fresh lime juice
    (about 6 limes)
⅔ cup / 150 ml elderflower cordial
scant ¼ cup / 50 ml sugar syrup
    (see page 10)
1¼ cups / 300 ml pomegranate juice
1¼ cups / 300 ml prosecco

Serves 10

Add all the ingredients to a pitcher filled with ice and stir gently to mix.

Serve in tall ice-filled glasses, garnished with the spent husks of the squeezed limes.

Sangria Classic

Everyone needs to know how to make a good Sangria, the good news
is that there are very few rules. So long as you add red wine (Spanish
Rioja is especially good) and some fruit, you shouldn't offend anyone.

1 x 75 cl bottle dry red wine
⅔ cup/150 ml Grand Marnier
1 cup/250 ml fresh orange juice
  (about 4 oranges)
scant ¼ cup/50 ml sugar syrup
  (see page 10)
3 dashes Angostura bitters
seasonal fresh fruit, to garnish

Serves 10

Add all the ingredients to a pitcher filled with ice and stir gently to mix.

Serve in ice-filled glasses, garnished with seasonal fruit.

Variation: For a special occasion, I recommend adding a 75 cl
bottle of Champagne to the punch bowl to give it extra fizz.

Blanco Sangria

The elderflower liqueur adds a wonderful floral note to this classic
summer drink and brings out the sweetness of the season's fruits.

1 x 75 cl bottle crisp dry white wine
⅖ cup/100 ml St Germain
  elderflower liqueur
⅖ cup/100 ml dry vermouth
⅖ cup/100 ml Cointreau
3 oz./80 ml fresh lemon juice
  (about 2 lemons)
generous oz./30 ml sugar syrup
  (see page 10), to taste
2 heavy dashes grapefruit bitters
seasonal fresh fruit, to garnish

Serves 10

Add all the ingredients to a pitcher filled with ice and stir gently to mix.

Serve in ice-filled glasses, garnished with seasonal fruit.

Summer Cocktails

These refreshing tipples are packed with fresh fruits and juices, quality liquors and all cooled down with plenty of ice. What more could you want on a hot summer's day?

Berry Caipiroska

Fresh berries not only give this refreshing cocktail a sweet fruitiness, but they also make a delightfully pretty drink to serve as an aperitif before an alfresco lunch.

2 oz./50 ml vodka
4 lime wedges
2 white sugar cubes
3 fresh berries (strawberries, raspberries, and blueberries are all good), plus extra to garnish

toothpicks/cocktail sticks

Serves 1

Muddle all the ingredients in a rock glass with a wooden pestle. Top up with crushed ice and stir gently to mix.

Serve garnished with a few fresh berries skewered onto a toothpick/cocktail stick.

FOR EXTRA ZING

The Caipiroska is an elegant twist on the classic Caipirinha, using vodka instead of the usual cachaça. If preferred, omit the berries and add extra lime for a more citrussy tipple.

Moscow Mule

Ginger beer is what gives a mule its easy spiciness and it works
beautifully here with zesty lime to create the perfect long drink
for a hot summer's day.

2 oz./50 ml vodka
4 lime wedges
spicy ginger beer, to top up

Serves 1

Add the vodka to a tall, ice-filled glass. Squeeze over the lime wedges
and drop the spent husks in too. Top up with ginger beer and serve.

Anejo Highball

"Rum, lime, and curaçao are the holy trinity of Caribbean cocktails."
So says legendary American bartender Dale de Groff, the creator
of this tribute to classic Cuban drinks.

2 oz./50 ml aged rum
½ oz./15 ml orange curaçao
½ oz./15 ml fresh lime juice
2 dashes Angostura bitters
ginger beer, to top up
an orange zest spiral, to garnish

Serves 1

Add all the ingredients to an ice-filled highball glass. Top up with
the ginger beer and stir gently to mix. Serve garnished with an orange
zest spiral.

Bermuda Rum Swizzle

The important thing about this cocktail is to make it so cold that the outside of the glass literally frosts up. This was originally achieved by "swizzling" the drink with a twig from the "swizzle stick tree" (see page 124). Crushed ice is essential to achieve this effect.

2 oz./50 ml Gosling's Black
   Seal rum
1 oz./25 ml fresh orange juice
1 oz./25 ml pineapple juice
½ oz./12.5 ml fresh lime juice
½ oz./12.5 ml Falernum
1 barspoon grenadine syrup
a dash of Angostura bitters
orange and pineapple slices, to garnish

Serves 1

Add all the ingredients to a highball glass filled with crushed ice.

Swizzle by placing a barspoon or small whisk into the glass and swizzling between the palms of your hands until frost appears on the outside of the glass.

Serve garnished with orange and pineapple slices.

Hurricane

This classic cocktail was created by Pat O'Brien in his New Orleans tavern in the 1940s. Try not to use the hurricane mix widely available but instead play with different brands of passion fruit syrup. You may want to add a splash of passion fruit juice too, if you want to make this drink feel like it's lasting longer.

2 oz./50 ml dark Jamaican rum
1 oz./25 ml fresh lemon juice
1 oz./25 ml passion fruit syrup
passion fruit juice (optional)
passion fruit seeds, to garnish

Serves 1

Add all the ingredients to a cocktail shaker filled with ice and shake vigorously to mix.

Strain into a Hurricane glass or Tiki mug filled with crushed ice, top up with passion fruit juice, if using, and serve garnished with passion fruit seeds.

Colonel Beach's Plantation Punch

Donn Beach, the godfather of the Tiki movement, liked to experiment
with more unusual ingredients in his punches—with fantastic results!

2 oz./50 ml gold Jamaican rum
1 oz./25 ml gold Cuban rum
1 oz./25 ml gold Barbadian rum
1 oz./25 ml fresh lime juice
2 oz./50 ml ginger beer
2 oz./50 ml pineapple juice
2 dashes Angostura bitters
2 dashes Falernum
2 dashes Pernod
an orange slice, cocktail cherry, and
    fresh mint sprig, to garnish

Serves 1

Add all the ingredients to a cocktail shaker filled with ice and shake
together to mix.

Pour into an ice-filled Tiki mug (if you have one) or glass, and serve
garnished with an orange slice, cocktail cherry, and a mint sprig.

Planter's Punch

As the title itself suggests, a Planter's Punch was the house punch consumed after a day's toil on Caribbean plantations. As a result, there aren't really any hard or fast rules as to what to include so long as you stick to the punch mantra of sour, sweet, strong, and weak.

2 oz./50 ml light Puerto
   Rican-style rum
2 oz./50 ml fresh orange juice
generous oz./30 ml fresh lemon juice
1 tablespoon/15 ml grenadine
1 oz./25 ml soda water
2 barspoons/10 ml dark
   Jamaican rum
an orange slice and cocktail cherry,
   to garnish

Serves 1

Add the light rum, orange and lemon juices, and grenadine to a cocktail shaker and shake together. Pour into a highball glass filled with crushed ice and top up with soda.

Gently pour the dark rum over the surface—it should float naturally on top. Serve garnished with an orange slice and a cocktail cherry.

The Knickerbocker

This is a great punch, reclaimed from the cocktail books of yester-year, that follows all the rules. You may want to have a play with the sweetness of this drink when you're adding the raspberry syrup, relative to your own personal taste.

2 oz./50 ml Santa Cruz rum
1 oz./25 ml orange curaçao
scant oz./20 ml fresh lemon juice
½ oz./15 ml fresh lime juice
fresh raspberries, to garnish

raspberry syrup
⅔ cup/150 ml sugar syrup
   (see page 10)
8 fresh raspberries

Serves 1

To make the raspberry syrup, put the raspberries in a mixing glass or bowl and press them gently with the back of a spoon to release the juice. Cover with sugar syrup and leave overnight to infuse. Pass the syrup through a fine mesh strainer and discard the raspberry pulp and seeds.

Add 2 barspoons of the raspberry syrup to a cocktail shaker with the rum and curaçao and fill with ice. Squeeze in the juice from the lemon and limes, and drop the spent husks in too. Shake the mixture together.

Strain the drink into a stemmed cocktail glass and serve garnished with fresh raspberries.

Queen's Park Swizzle

This drink is a kind of hybrid between the daiquiri and the mojito. The key to the intense flavor is to use a heavier sugar syrup, made from less-refined demerera sugar, which compliments the fuller style of rum.

2 oz./50 ml Guyanese rum
    (El Dorado 12 yr is amazing)
scant oz./20 ml fresh lime juice
½ oz./15 ml dark sugar syrup
    (see page 10, substituting the
    superfine/caster sugar for
    half demerera and half dark
    muscovado sugar)
2 dashes Angostura bitters
5 fresh mint leaves, plus a mint sprig,
    to garnish

Add the rum, lime juice, sugar syrup, Angostura bitters, and mint leaves to a highball glass filled with crushed ice. Swizzle by placing a barspoon or small whisk into the glass and swizzling between the palms of your hands until frost appears on the outside of the glass.

Serve garnished with half a spent lime husk and a mint sprig.

Serves 1

Hemingway Daiquiri

This classy cocktail is a slightly tarter version of the daiquiri.
The inclusion of maraschino liqueur adds length and mouth-feel
to the drink. Don't overdo it though—that dry cherry flavor should
sneak onto your palate right at the last moment.

2 oz./50 ml light Puerto
    Rican-style rum
scant oz./20 ml fresh grapefruit juice
2 barspoons/10 ml fresh lime juice
2 barspoons/10 ml maraschino
    liqueur
pared lemon zest, to garnish

Serves 1

Add all the ingredients to a cocktail shaker filled with ice and shake
sharply to mix.

Strain into a chilled coupette glass and serve garnished with lemon zest.

Commodore cocktail

Many people ask me what egg white adds to the flavor of a drink.
Flavor is made up of not just taste and aroma, but also mouth-feel
and appearance. That light frothy cloud that sits on the cocktail's
surface not only makes the drink look fantastic but will lend it
a fluffy lightness that helps it slip down smoothly.

2 oz. / 50 ml light Puerto
  Rican-style rum
1 oz. / 25 ml fresh lemon juice
2 barspoons / 10 ml grenadine
2 barspoons / 10 ml raspberry syrup
  (see page 60)
1 barspoon superfine / caster sugar
1 egg white

Serves 1

Add all ingredients to a cocktail shaker filled with ice and shake sharply
to blend and whip up the egg white.

Strain into a frosted coupette glass and serve immediately while the
froth is still at it's best.

Missionary's Downfall

This is one of my favorite Tiki drinks. The rum, mint, pineapple, peach, and crushed ice combine to create a deliciously refreshing tipple. Some people insist on shaking this drink and straining the mint fragments out through a strainer; I always stick with the blended version as this allows the mint to marry well with the fresh pineapple slice.

50 ml light *Puerto Rican-style rum*
½ oz. / 15 ml *peach brandy*
½ *pineapple ring*
1½ oz. / 40 ml *fresh lime juice*
4 *fresh mint sprigs*
1 *barspoon / 5 ml sugar syrup*
  (see page 10)
orange slices and a fresh mint sprig,
  to garnish

Serves 1

Add all the ingredients to a blender with 1 scoop of crushed ice and blitz until smooth.

Pour into an ice-filled highball glass and serve garnished with orange slices and a mint sprig.

Hedgerow Sling

Here's a cocktail that with the right amount of care and attention can look as good as it tastes. Drizzle the crème de mure gently into the drink, right at the end, to create a beautiful marbled effect.

1 oz./25 ml gin
1 oz./25 ml sloe gin
1 oz./25 ml fresh lemon juice
2 barspoons/10 ml sugar syrup
  (see page 10)
⅓ cup/100 ml soda water
2 barspoons/10 ml crème de mure
seasonal fresh berries and a slice of
  lemon, to garnish

Serves 1

Add the gin, sloe gin, lemon juice, and sugar syrup to a cocktail shaker filled with ice and shake together. Strain into a sling glass filled with crushed ice.

Top up with soda water and drizzle over the crème de mure. Serve garnished with seasonal berries and a slice of lemon.

Garrick Gin Punch

If the dryness of a good London gin is your thing then this is your cocktail. A superb aperitif, this cocktail will cut through the fug of your day and prepare your palate for whatever the evening holds. Shake it until it's as cold as it can be and serve in a chilled glass.

2 oz./50 ml London dry gin
1 oz./25 ml fresh lemon juice
½ oz./12.5 ml maraschino liqueur
a dash of sugar syrup
    (see page 10)
2 dashes Angostura bitters
lemon zest, to garnish

Serves 1

Add all the ingredients to a cocktail shaker filled with ice and shake together until the outside of the shaker starts to frost.

Strain into a frosted coupette glass and serve garnished with a thin piece of lemon zest.

Jalisco Siesta

This crisp, refreshing punch is a variation of the mojito using tequila instead of rum and "twisting" all the other ingredients. The herbaceous, slightly vegetal aroma of the tequila combines well with the mint and its spiciness is perfectly matched to the ginger beer.

1 oz./25 ml fresh lemon juice
½ oz./15 ml agave syrup
5 fresh mint leaves
2 oz./50 ml reposado tequila
2 oz./50 ml ginger beer
large fresh mint sprigs, to garnish

Serves 1

Add the lemon juice, agave syrup, and mint leaves to a highball glass and muddle gently.

Fill the glass with crushed ice and add the tequila and ginger beer. Stir gently to mix and serve garnished with a mint sprig.

Air Mail

There's nothing like adding some bubbly to a cocktail to lend the drink a celebratory feel. Make sure you stir the honey into the other ingredients well before adding ice or it will harden inside your shaker and not mix properly with the other ingredients.

1 oz./25 ml gold Puerto
   Rican-style rum
½ oz./12.5 ml fresh lime juice
1 barspoon/5 ml honey
Champagne, to top up

Serves 1

Add the rum, lime juice, and honey to a cocktail shaker and stir until the honey is dissolved. Add ice and shake to mix.

Strain into a Champagne flute, top up with Champagne, and serve.

Peach Blossom Spring

This is a slight deviation of the classic Bellini, adding a little extra kick with the vodka and peach liqueur. Perfect for serving on a summer's evening or before a dinner party to get the night's proceeding off to a sophisticated start.

1 oz./25 ml vodka
1 oz./25 ml peach purée
2 barspoons/10 ml crème de peche
prosecco, to top up
2 dashes peach bitters
a peach slice, to garnish

Serves 1

Add the vodka, peach purée, and crème de peche to a cocktail shaker filled with ice and shake to mix.

Strain into a champagne flute and top up with prosecco. Add two dashes of peach bitters and serve garnished with a fresh peach slice.

Holiday Punches

On a chilly winter's day, one of these classic winter warmers is perfect to serve by the fireside. Full of the rich flavors of spices, wine, and fall fruits, these drinks are guaranteed to delight.

Harvest Punch

If this delicious winter warmer doesn't have enough bite to keep out the cold, try adding a measure of Calvados apple brandy. Be aware that some brands of cider are sweeter than others, so you may want to adjust the amount of sugar you add to balance it out.

4 cups / 1 litre hard apple cider
1½ cups / 300 g brown sugar
1 teaspoon allspice
1 teaspoon ground nutmeg
1 teaspoon ground cinnamon
apple slices studded with cloves,
*   to garnish*

Serves 6

Add all the ingredients to a saucepan set over medium heat and simmer gently for 1 hour, stirring frequently.

Remove from the heat and pour into a heat-resistant punch bowl. Serve in heat-resistant punch cups or glasses, garnished with apple slices studded with cloves.

Baltimore Eggnog

In essence, eggnog is a mixture of cream (or milk), sugar, and beaten
egg that can have alcohol added to it. Of the many variations around,
Baltimore eggnog is my favorite: three different types of liquor as well
as the dusting of spice really add extra depth.

1 oz./25 ml Madeira wine
½ oz./12.5 ml Cognac
½ oz./12.5 ml Jamaican rum
a pinch of ground cinnamon
1 tablespoon superfine/caster sugar
1 egg
1 oz./25 ml heavy/double cream
grated nutmeg, to serve

Serves 1

Add all the ingredients to a cocktail shaker and shake vigorously
for 15 seconds.

Pour into glasses and grate over a little nutmeg, to serve.

Mulled Wine

Traditionally made with red wine, sugar, and spices, this drink is always served hot. Try not to let your mixture boil when you heat it as this may impair the flavor.

2 x 75 cl bottles red wine
⅓ cup / 100 ml brandy
pared zest and freshly squeezed juice
   of 2 clementines
pared zest of one lime
pared zest of one lemon
1 cup / 200 g superfine / caster sugar
1 cinnamon stick
4 cloves
4 pinches of grated nutmeg
1 split vanilla bean / pod
lemon zest and cinnamon sticks,
   to garnish

Serves 10

Add all the ingredients to a large saucepan set over medium heat. Simmer gently for about 30 minutes, stirring occasionally.

Serve in heatproof glasses garnished with extra lemon zest and cinnamon sticks.

The Hot Toddy

For some reason this drink is often only consumed when the drinker feels under the weather, but the hot toddy is my winter warmer of choice. It's perfect for sipping after any outdoor activity when things have turned frosty.

2 oz./50 ml Scotch whisky
scant 1 oz./20 ml dark honey
1 oz./25 ml fresh lemon juice
a pinch of ground cinnamon
    or 1 cinnamon stick
boiling water, to top up
2 pieces of lemon zest, studded
    with cloves, to garnish

Serves 1

Add all the ingredients to a heatproof glass or pewter tankard and stir gently to mix. Top up with boiling water and serve garnished with a piece of lemon zest studded with cloves.

Negus

There always seems to be plenty of port around during the festive season, and rightly so. I could happily while away the hours after dinner, begrudgingly passing the bottle to my left. But if you're looking for something more complex for your port, look no further than the Negus.

3 oz./75 ml Tawny port
1 oz./25 ml fresh lemon juice
2 barspoons/10 ml sugar syrup
  (see page 10)
boiling water, to top up
lemon zest, to garnish
grated nutmeg, to serve

Serves 1

Add the port, sugar, and lemon juice to a heat-resistant glass and stir gently to mix. Top up with boiling water and serve garnished with a piece of lemon zest and a dusting of nutmeg.

Hot Buttered Rum

Rum may be the perfect ingredient for a summer Carribean-style cocktail, but it also happily lends itself to those winter nights, with the sweetness of the rum combining with the spices and the brown sugar. Try also adding cinnamon or vanilla to the mix for added complexity.

3 teaspoons brown sugar
2 oz./50 ml dark rum
½ teaspoon allspice
1 teaspoon butter
hot water, to top up
a piece of orange zest studded
* with cloves, to garnish*

Serves 1

Warm a heat-resistant glass and add the sugar and a little hot water. Stir until the sugar has dissolved and then add the rum, allspice, and butter. Top up with hot water and stir until the butter has melted.

Garnish with a piece of orange zest studded with cloves, and serve.

Sherry Cobbler

The Sherry Cobbler was one of "the" cocktails of the 19th century. Delightfully smooth, this cocktail calls for a smattering of fresh berries to garnish, but I prefer it toned down to its bare essentials with just a curl of lemon zest. There is evidence to suggest that this was one of the first cocktails to utilize a reed to act as... yup, you've guessed it, a straw.

2 cups / 500 ml Amontillado sherry
⅓ cup / 100 ml fresh lemon juice
   (about 2½ lemons)
⅓ cup / 100 ml fresh orange juice
   (about 2 oranges)
⅓ cup / 100 ml sugar syrup
   (see page 10)
⅔ cup / 150 ml pineapple purée
lemon and orange zest, to garnish

Serves 10

Add all the ingredients to a punch bowl filled with ice and stir gently to mix.

Serve in punch cups or glasses filled with cracked ice and garnish with pieces of lemon or orange zest.

Non-alcoholic Refreshers

If you are catering for a large group of people, it is always good to provide some non-alcoholic options. These cocktails may lack alcohol, but they certainly don't lack taste.

Fresh Watermelon & Cinnamon Punch

Take my word for it on this one, watermelon and cinnamon do work well together! In fact, the delicate flavor of watermelon works well with many herbs and spices, including chile, mint, and even rosemary.

2 large watermelons, peeled and roughly chopped
1 cup/250 ml fresh lime juice (about 8 limes)
sparkling mineral water, to top up

cinnamon-infused syrup
2 cups/400 g sugar
a pinch of ground cinnamon

Serves 10

To make the cinnamon syrup, put the sugar, cinnamon, and 1 cup/250 ml water in a saucepan set over low heat. Heat gently, stirring until the sugar has dissolved. Remove from the heat and leave to stand for at least 2 hours.

Put the watermelon in a blender with the lime juice, ¾ cup/200 ml of cinnamon syrup, and 1 scoop crushed ice. Blend until smooth. (You may have to blend the watermelon in batches if it all won't fit in the blender at once.)

Pour the watermelon mixture into a punch bowl and add a block of ice. Top up with sparkling mineral water, stir, and serve.

English Summer Punch

Apples and cherries are a great flavor pairing and have been combined in desserts with great results over the years. The good news is, they work as well in a punch as they do in a cobbler or a crumble.

6 cups / 1.5 litres cloudy apple juice
½ cup / 125 ml fresh lime juice
    (about 4 limes)
200 ml / ¾ cup sparkling mineral
    water, to top up
10 fresh cherries, to garnish

cherry-infused syrup
1 cup / 125 g cherries, pitted
400 g / 2 cups sugar

Serves 10

To make the cherry syrup, put the cherries in a blender and blitz for 1 minute. Put the blended cherries, sugar, and 1 cup / 250 ml water in a saucepan set over low heat. Heat gently, stirring frequently, until the sugar is dissolved. Remove from the heat and leave to cool.

Add the cherry syrup, apple juice, lime juice, and mineral water to a large punch bowl filled with ice and stir gently to mix.

Serve in tall, ice-filled glasses, garnished with fresh cherries.

Strawberry & Mint Lemonade

I've never understood why people prefer to buy lemonade when it's
so easy to make at home. Freshly made lemonade combined with fresh
blended strawberries and decorated with a mint sprig is as pleasant
an assault on the nostrils as one can imagine.

20 ripe strawberries
⅔ cup / 160 ml fresh lemon juice
  (about 4 lemons)
grated zest of 4 lemons
6 tablespoons superfine / caster sugar
1 large handful of fresh mint
soda water, to top
mint sprigs, to garnish

Serves 2

Put the strawberries in a blender and blitz to a purée.

Add the lemon juice and zest, sugar, and mint to a large pitcher
and stir until the sugar has dissolved. Fill the pitcher with ice, add
the blended strawberries, and top up with soda water.

Serve in ice-filled highball glasses, garnished with a mint sprig.

Homemade Cola Cordial

Okay, you may argue that nothing quite beats the "real thing", but
trust me there's something quite rewarding about "cracking" the
recipe and sipping smugly on your own homemade version.

1 cup/200 g granulated sugar
1 cup/200 g dark muscovado sugar
1 vanilla bean/pod, seeded
1 cinnamon stick
a pinch of nutmeg
pared zest of 1 orange
pared zest of 1 lemon
pared zest of 1 lime
¾ cup/200 ml carbonated water
    per glass, to serve
pared citrus zest, to garnish

Makes about ¾ cup/200 ml

Put the granulated and muscovado sugar and 2 cups/500 ml of water
in a large saucepan set over medium heat. Simmer gently, stirring
frequently, until the sugar has dissolved. Turn down the heat and add
the vanilla bean/pod, cinnamon, nutmeg, and the zests of the citrus
fruit. Allow to simmer for 2 hours over a low heat, stirring occasionally,
until it has reduced to a thin syrup. Leave the cordial to cool and then
pass though a strainer and set aside until needed.

Add the desired amount (relative to sweetness of tooth) to an ice-filled
highball glass and top up with ¾ cup/200 ml of carbonated water.
Serve garnished with pieces of citrus zest.

Note: If you are not using the cordial immediately, decant into
a bottle and store in the refrigerator—it will keep for up to 2 days.

Tropical Punch

**When making punches that involve whole fruits or fruit juices, always
try and use the fresh fruit and juice or blend it, rather than using
ingredients from cartons—the result will be far superior.**

*2 large ripe mangos, peeled, pitted,
and roughly chopped*
*2 slices pineapple, peeled, cored, and
roughly chopped*
*1⅔ cups / 400 ml fresh pink grapefruit
juice (about 4 grapefruits)*
generous oz. / 30 ml fresh lime juice
1-inch / 2.5-cm piece fresh ginger, peeled
*scant ¼ cup / 50 ml sugar syrup
(see page 10)*
mineral water to thin (still or sparkling)
pineapple leaves, to garnish

Add all the ingredients to a blender with 1 scoop crushed ice and
blitz until smooth.

Pour into ice-filled glasses and top up with mineral water to loosen
the mixture, if required. Serve garnished with pineapple leaves.

Serves 2

Citrus Fizz

As the name suggests, this is quite a sour drink. If your taste buds crave
something sweeter, you may want to add a dash of sugar syrup or try
using a different flavor sorbet. The sorbet should keep the drink nice
and cold as it melts.

4 cups/I litre fresh blood orange juice
　(about 17 oranges)
1 cup/250 ml fresh pink grapefruit
　juice (about 2½ grapefruits)
⅓ cup/100 ml fresh lemon juice
　(about 2½ lemons)
8 scoops lemon sorbet
superfine/caster sugar, to taste
soda water, to top up

Serves 6

Strain the freshly squeezed juices into a punch bowl with a small block
of ice. Add the sorbet and a sprinkling of sugar and stir gently to mix.

Serve in punch cups or glasses topped up with soda water.

Triple Goddess

Pomegranate, apple, elderflower, and lime combine to create a tangy effervescence in this "mocktail". Try to find a pomegranate juice that errs on the slightly bitter side and the drink will balance perfectly, offset by the sweetness of the apple juice and elderflower.

⅔ cup / 150 ml pomegranate juice
⅔ cup / 150 ml cloudy apple juice
1½ oz. / 40 ml freshly squeezed
   lime juice (about 1½ limes)
1 oz. / 25 ml elderflower cordial
sparkling mineral water, to top up
an apple fan, to garnish

Serves 2

Add the fruit juices and elderflower cordial to an ice-filled highball glass and stir gently to mix.

Top up with the mineral water and serve garnished with an apple fan.

Tiki Breeze

Pineapple and mint are generally regarded as integral ingredients of the Tiki cocktail. Add fresh ginger, peach, and orange to this and not only have you got an authentic Tiki drink, but one with a subtle depth of taste that has all the goodness that a non-alcoholic cocktail can provide.

5 pineapples, peeled, cored, and
* roughly chopped*
2 peaches, pitted but unpeeled
5 cups / 1.25 litres fresh orange juice
* (about 20 oranges)*
a small handful of fresh mint leaves
3-4-inch / 8-10-cm piece fresh
* ginger, peeled*

Serves 10

Add all the ingredients to a blender with 1 scoop of crushed ice and blitz for 15 seconds. Pour into an ice-filled pitcher.

Serve in ice-filled highball glasses.

Light Bites

When serving drinks, it's always a good idea to have some light bites to serve alongside. These delicious morsels are the ideal fingerfood, and perfectly compliment the flavors of the cocktails.

Marinated Olives

1 lb. / 500 g black Spanish olives,
  drained with brine reserved
4 garlic cloves, sliced
2 dried red chiles
8 black peppercorns
1 slice of lemon
4 sprigs of fresh parsley
4 fresh bay leaves
a pinch of salt
1¼ cups / 300 ml red wine vinegar

Serves 4

Put the olives in a bowl. Mix in the garlic, chiles, pepper, lemon, parsley, bay leaves, and salt, then transfer to a jar into which they just fit. Pour over the vinegar and the reserved brine. Shake well and let marinate at room temperature for 2 weeks.

Variation: To marinate green olives, add 2 extra garlic cloves to the marinade and replace the chiles and other ingredients with 1 tablespoon crushed coriander seeds, 1 tablespoon crushed fennel seeds, 6 fresh thyme sprigs, 4 fresh rosemary sprigs, and the grated zest and freshly squeezed juice of 1 orange. Cover with olive oil and marinate for 6 days.

Spicy Cajun Mixed Nuts

5½ oz. / 150 g unsalted cashews
5½ oz. / 150 g pecans
5 oz. / 140 g pistachios
1 teaspoon cayenne pepper
1 teaspoon smoked paprika
  (pimentón)
½ teaspoon dried thyme
1 tablespoon soft brown sugar
1 teaspoon fine sea salt
1 tablespoon olive oil

a baking sheet lined with baking
  parchment

Serves 10-12

Preheat the oven to 350°F (180°C) Gas 4.

Put all of the nuts in a large bowl. Add the cayenne pepper, paprika, thyme, sugar, and salt and mix to combine. Stir in the olive oil. Tip the nuts out onto the prepared baking sheet, spreading them out into a single layer.

Bake in the preheated oven for 10 minutes, stirring about halfway through the cooking time. Let cool completely before spooning into serving bowls. They will keep in an airtight container for 7–10 days.

Crab Toasts with Chive, Caper, & Radish Salsa

Present a few of these toasts with the salsa on top as they look so pretty. Fresh crab is delicious in its own right, so serve the rest of the salsa in a bowl with a small serving spoon so your guests can add as much or little as they wish.

1 slim baguette
1 lb./500 g fresh lump crabmeat
7 oz./200 g fromage frais

For the salsa:
7 oz./200 g tiny radishes
 (French breakfast, if available),
 roughly chopped
½ cup/70 g capers, drained
 and chopped
½ cup/40 g finely chopped fresh chives
4 tablespoons olive oil
4 tablespoons ginger wine (such
 as Stone's) or sweet sherry plus
 ¼ teaspoon ground ginger

2 baking sheets

Makes 40

Preheat the oven to 400°F (200°C) Gas 6.

Slice the baguette into 40 even slices and arrange in a single layer on the baking sheets. Bake in the preheated oven for about 10 minutes, until nicely browned.

Gently combine the fresh crabmeat and fromage frais in a bowl and chill. When you are ready to serve, mix all the salsa ingredients together in a separate bowl. Use a small palette knife to spread the cold crab mixture onto the toasts, then top with a little salsa. Serve immediately.

Twice-marinated Salt Lime Chicken

Something magical happens when you put lime and salt together. Whet guests' appetites with this zingy, salty chicken canapé. These are perfect served with tequila-based cocktails, such as the Lahara Margarita on page 39 or the Paloma Punch on page 36.

1 lb./500 g skinless, boneless
chicken thighs
3 tablespoons olive oil
grated zest and freshly squeezed juice
of 2 unwaxed limes
a generous pinch of salt crystals

non-metallic shallow dish
toothpicks/cocktail sticks
   or small forks

Makes 40

Cut the chicken into 40 even chunks and put them in a non-metallic dish with 1 tablespoon of the olive oil, the zest and juice of 1 of the limes, and half the salt crystals. Let marinate in the fridge for 2 hours.

When you are ready to cook, remove the chicken from the marinade. Heat the remaining olive oil in a skillet and sauté the chicken over medium heat for about 5 minutes until cooked through, shaking the skillet occasionally. Put in a clean dish with the remaining salt and lime zest and juice. Mix and chill for 1 hour before serving with toothpicks/ cocktail sticks or small forks.

Gingery Chicken Tikka Skewers with Minted Yogurt

2 lbs. / 900 g chicken breasts,
   cut into bite-size pieces
2 tablespoons ghee or butter, melted

For the marinade:
1¾ cups / 450 ml thick plain yogurt,
   left to drain through cheesecloth /
   muslin for 1–2 hours
1½ oz. / 40 g fresh ginger, peeled
   and pounded to a pulp
2–3 garlic cloves, crushed
2 teaspoons chili powder
2 teaspoons ground cinnamon
2 teaspoons ground cumin
1 teaspoon ground coriander
1 teaspoon ground cardamom
1 teaspoon ground cloves
1 teaspoon ground black pepper
1–2 teaspoons sea salt
freshly squeezed juice of 1 lemon

For the minted yogurt:
6 tablespoons thick plain yogurt
freshly squeezed juice of ½ a lemon
2 garlic cloves, crushed
sea salt and freshly ground
   black pepper
leaves from a small bunch of fresh mint,
   finely chopped or shredded

a package of short wooden or bamboo
   skewers, soaked in water before use

Serves 4-6

This version of the classic Indian tikka is incredibly versatile as you can vary the spices according to your taste. Serve the tasty little bits of chicken with this refreshing minted yogurt or your favorite fruit chutney.

To prepare the marinade, beat together the strained yogurt, ginger, and garlic then stir in the spices and lemon juice. Toss the chicken pieces in the marinade, making sure they are thoroughly coated. Cover, refrigerate, and leave to marinate for at least 2 hours.

Meanwhile, prepare the minted yogurt. Beat the yogurt with the lemon juice and garlic. Season to taste and stir in the mint. Set aside.

Thread the chicken onto the prepared skewers, leaving behind any excess marinade, and brush the melted ghee over them. Prepare a charcoal grill/barbecue or heat the broiler/grill. Cook the skewers for about 3 minutes on each side, until the chicken is nicely browned and cooked through. Serve with the minted yogurt on the side for dipping.

Spicy Beef and Coconut Kofta Kabobs

Variations of these wonderfully aromatic kabobs can be found at street stalls from Sri Lanka to the Philippines and South Africa to the West Indies. Simple and tasty, the kofta are delicious served with wedges of fresh lime or a dipping sauce of your choice. The exotic flavor of coconut makes them a perfect companion to any Tiki punch.

1 teaspoon coriander seeds

1 teaspoon cumin seeds

1⅓ cups / 100 g shredded / desiccated or freshly grated coconut, plus extra to serve

1 tablespoon coconut oil

4 shallots, peeled and finely chopped

2 garlic cloves, finely chopped

1–2 fresh red chiles, seeded and finely chopped

12 oz. / 350 g lean ground beef

1 beaten egg, to bind

sea salt and freshly ground black pepper

lime wedges, to serve

a package of short wooden or bamboo skewers, soaked in water before use

Serves 4

In a small heavy-based skillet, dry roast the coriander and cumin seeds until they give off a nutty aroma. Using a mortar and pestle, or a spice grinder, grind the roasted seeds to a powder.

In the same skillet, dry roast the coconut until it begins to color and give off a nutty aroma. Tip it onto a plate to cool.

Heat the coconut oil in the same small heavy-based skillet and stir in the shallots, garlic, and chiles, until fragrant and beginning to color. Tip them onto a plate to cool.

Put the ground beef in a bowl and add the ground spices, toasted coconut, and shallot mixture. Season with salt and pepper and use a fork to mix all the ingredients together, adding a little egg to bind it (you may not need it all). Knead the mixture with your hands and mold it into little balls. Thread the balls onto the prepared skewers.

Prepare a charcoal grill/barbecue or heat the broiler/grill. Cook the kabobs for 2–3 minutes on each side. Sprinkle the cooked kofta with the toasted coconut and serve with the wedges of lime for guests to squeeze over them.

Phyllo Cigars with Halloumi

Fried in a little oil, phyllo pastry cooks to a lovely golden crisp. These freeze well (laid between sheets of baking parchment) and can be cooked from frozen, making them perfect for parties or impromptu drinks.

4 sheets of phyllo pastry, thawed
    if frozen
7 oz./200 g halloumi cheese, grated
2 oz./50 g feta cheese, crumbled
1 stick/125 g butter, melted
    and cooled
½ cup/80 g pitted and sliced
    black olives
16 small fresh mint leaves
light olive oil, for frying

a baking sheet lined with baking
    parchment

Makes 16

Cut each sheet of phyllo pastry in half lengthwise. Stack them on top of each other, then cover with a large piece of baking parchment. Place a damp dish towel on top of the parchment to prevent the phyllo from drying out.

Combine the halloumi and feta in a bowl. Lay a sheet of phyllo on a clean work surface with one of the short ends nearest to you. Lightly brush all over with melted butter. Spoon 1 tablespoon of the cheese mixture on the end of the phyllo, about ½ inch/1 cm from the edge, and use your fingers to mold it into a small log. Top with 2–3 slices of olive and a few mint leaves. Roll over the edge nearest to you to enclose the filling, then fold in the sides. Brush the folded-down sides with a little butter, then roll up quite tightly to form a small, cigar-shaped package. Repeat to make 16 cigars, putting them on the prepared baking sheet as you go.

Set a skillet over high heat and brush with a little oil. Cook the phyllo cigars for 2–3 minutes, turning often, until they are golden brown and crisp. Serve warm.

Warm Spice-rubbed Potatoes with Rosemary Mayonnaise

This recipe uses pink-skinned new potatoes for their charming color and firm texture. If they're not available, you can substitute any large potatoes, peeled and cut to your preferred size. These warm bites are perfect for serving with any of the Holiday Punches.

For the mayonnaise:
3 egg yolks
3 tablespoons fresh rosemary needles
1 teaspoon Dijon mustard
3 tablespoons cider vinegar
2 cups / 500 ml grapeseed oil

For the potatoes:
1½ lbs. / 750 g pink-skinned new
    potatoes, halved lengthwise
1 teaspoon cayenne pepper
1 teaspoon caraway seeds
1 teaspoon coriander seeds
a small piece of cinnamon stick
1 garlic clove, crushed
1 teaspoon sea salt
2 tablespoons olive oil

toothpicks/cocktail sticks or
    small forks

Serves 12

To make the mayonnaise, put all the ingredients, except the grapeseed oil, in a food processor and blend. With the motor running, slowly add the oil in droplets until the mayonnaise starts to thicken. Continue with an even trickle until you have incorporated all the oil. Spoon into a bowl and chill.

For the potatoes, cook the potatoes in a large pan of boiling water for about 12–15 minutes, until almost cooked. Drain and pat dry.

Preheat the oven to 400°F (200°C) Gas 6.

Gently warm the spices in a small pan for about 2 minutes until their scent starts to pervade the kitchen. Put the warmed spices, garlic, and salt in the clean food processor and blend to make a rough spice mix.

Put the potatoes in a bowl with the olive oil and toss together. Using clean hands, rub the spice mixture onto the potatoes and bake them on a baking sheet in the preheated oven for about 20 minutes until golden. Serve with the rosemary mayonnaise, for dipping.

Polenta Fries with Green Tabasco Mayonnaise

These fries are perfect for serving at gatherings. The polenta makes a welcome change from the usual potato, and is the perfect vessel for the tangy Tabasco mayonnaise.

For the mayonnaise:
½ cup / 125 ml real mayonnaise
2 teaspoons green Tabasco sauce

For the polenta fries:
4 cups / 1 litre chicken or
    vegetable stock
⅔ cup / 250 g instant polenta
    or fine cornmeal
2 tablespoons butter
½ cup / 50 g finely grated
    Parmesan cheese
1 cup / 250 ml vegetable oil
½ cup / 125 ml light olive oil
3 tablespoons / 30 g all-purpose /
    plain flour

2 baking sheets, lightly greased

Makes about 60

Put the stock in a saucepan and bring to a boil. While the stock is boiling, pour in the polenta in a steady stream and whisk until it is all incorporated. Continue whisking for about 2 minutes, until the mixture is smooth and thickened. Remove from the heat and stir through the butter and Parmesan until well combined. Spoon half of the mixture into each of the baking sheets. Use the back of a metal spoon to smooth the top. Cover and refrigerate for at least 4 hours, until firm. Transfer the polenta to a chopping board. Trim the edges. Cut the blocks lengthwise in half, then cut into ½-inch / 1-cm thick slices, to make about 60 fries.

Pour the oils into a skillet and heat over medium/high heat. The oil is ready if a small piece of the polenta mixture sizzles on contact. Put about one quarter of the fries in a colander and sprinkle over some of the flour. Shake the colander to coat the fries in the flour and to remove the excess. Add these to the oil and cook for 4–5 minutes, turning often, until golden. Transfer the cooked fries to some paper towels to absorb the excess oil. Cover with foil and keep warm in a low oven while you cook the second batch. Repeat with the other fries.

Combine the mayonnaise and Tabasco in a bowl to serve alongside the hot fries for dipping.

Glossary

Agave syrup A syrup made from the same raw ingredient as Tequila. Very sweet but lower on the glycemic index, this syrup works particularly well with Tequila.

Bacardi A well-known brand of rum, which originated in Cuba in the 19th century. The company now produces a range of different rums, but the Bacardi name is synonymous with its original white rum.

Barspoon The barspoon measures a flat 5 ml measure. The long handle makes it the perfect tool for swizzling (rotating the spoon quickly between your palms to chill and muddle a drink quickly).

Benedictine A brandy based liqueur created in 1510 to revive tired monks, made with 27 different herbs, roots, spices, and sugar.

Bitters A potent herbal or fruit-flavored alcoholic essence added to drinks in tiny amounts for its distinctive flavor. The original and most widely used bitters, Angostura, was first produced in the 1820s and is now produced in Trinidad. It has a rum base and is flavored with herbs, but details of the recipe are a closely guarded secret. Orange bitters is flavored with orange peel and other botanicals; peach bitters is another type that is available.

Blending A cocktail-making technique, which involves combining ingredients using an electric blender.

Botanicals Fruits, herbs, and spices (for example, juniper berries, citrus zest, cardamom, angelica, and coriander seeds) widely used as flavorings in the manufacture of various spirits.

Bourbon See "Whiskey."

Brandy An alcoholic spirit distilled from grape wine (ordinary brandy) or from a fermented mash of fruit (fruit brandy, like peach and cherry brandy). Fruit brandy is also known as eau de vie and tends to be unaged. True brandy is produced in every wine-growing region of the world, but the best comes from France—for example, Cognac and Armagnac.

Building A cocktail-making technique, which involves pouring the liquid ingredients into a glass (invariably with ice) one at a time.

Cachaça A Brazilian spirit distilled directly from the juice of sugar cane.

Calvados An aged French apple brandy from Normandy.

Cider A fermented alcoholic beverage made from apples, sometimes called hard cider in the US.

Champagne A sparkling wine from the Champagne region of France. Sparkling wines produced elsewhere by the same method are labeled "Méthode Champenoise" and include cava (which is Spanish), spumante (Italian), and sekt (German).

Coconut cream/milk Ingredients derived from fresh coconut, used in cooking as well as for cocktails.

Cognac A high-quality French brandy from the Cognac region in the southwest of France, first produced in the 19th century.

Cointreau Made in France using a neutral grain spirit base, flavored with bitter and sweet orange peel sourced from all over the world, and sweetened.

Cordial In the UK, a cordial is a fruit concentrate, or syrup, usually diluted with water before being drunk. Elderflower cordial is made from the flowers of the elderflower tree; Rose's lime juice, the best-known brand of lime cordial, is made from West Indian limes. See also "Liqueur."

Crème de cassis A sweet liqueur of French origin made from blackcurrants, often simply referred to as "cassis."

Crème de mure A liqueur made from wild blackberries, often interchangeable with Chambord.

Crème de pêche A liqueur made from peaches.

Curaçao An orange-flavored liqueur of Caribbean origin, available in colorless, blue, orange, and green versions.

Earl Grey Tea was often used as the "weak" ingredient in punches. Where a recipe calls for black tea, Earl Grey will do the job.

Edging A cocktail-garnishing technique, which involves decorating the rim of a glass with a flavoring such as salt, sugar, cocoa powder, or grated nutmeg.

Falernum A clove, almond, and lime-flavored liqueur from Barbados (22 proof).

Fruit juice A soft drink made from fruit concentrate, water, and sugar, or juice that has been freshly extracted from fruit. Stick to the type of juice the recipe calls for—a carton of juice is no substitute for freshly squeezed fruit juice, nor vice versa.

Gin In a number of 19th century punch recipes, where the cocktail calls for the inclusion of gin, it may well be referring to Old Tom gin or Genever. Old Tom is a gin that predated London dry and was traditionally sweeter than its descendant. Genever is the Dutch variant and is made from grain and malt and flavored with juniper.

Ginger beer A slightly alcoholic drink made from fermented ginger root.

Grand Marnier A Cognac-based, orange-flavored French liqueur.

Grenadine A sweet, red non-alcoholic syrup, originally made from pomegranates but now often artificially flavored.

Liqueur Known also as "cordial" in the US, liqueurs are high-quality sweet spirits flavored with the fruits, seeds, leaves, or flowers of plants.

Maraschino A non-alcoholic syrup flavored with cherries.

Maraschino liqueur A sweet colorless liqueur made from maraska cherries.

Muddling A cocktail-making technique which involves using a barspoon or muddler to mash ingredients such as fruit and herbs in the bottom of a glass, so as to release their flavor.

Orgeat A milky non-alcoholic syrup flavored with almonds.

Overproof Any spirit which is described as overproof will have an ABV of no less than 57.2%. In this book overproof refers to rum. My preferred overproof rum is Wray and Nephew, a traditionally pot-stilled rum from Jamaica.

Pernod A French anise-flavored spirit, which turns a cloudy pale yellow when mixed with water.

Pisco A colorless South American spirit, distilled from the muscat grape and produced in Peru and Chile.

Port A fortified wine made in the same way as sherry and available in several styles; for example, tawny, ruby, vintage, and white. Originally made only in Portugal, port is now produced in countries such as Australia, America, and South Africa.

Proof The strength of an alcoholic liquor as defined in the USA; to convert from ABV to proof simply double the amount.

Prosecco A light sparkling wine from Italy that is popular with bartenders as a cheaper (but just as tasty) version of Champagne.

Rum A spirit distilled from molasses or directly from the fermented juices of sugar cane. There are hundreds of different rums, ranging in hue from light/white (colorless), through golden colors, to dark brown. The majority of rums are produced in the Caribbean. In this book, different styles of rum are referred to:
Puerto Rican—a light unaged rum, invariably column distilled.
Jamaican—a heavier rum, often pot stilled.

Santa Cruz—this would depend on the era your recipe comes from. Pre-prohibition would have been pot stilled, whereas after the 1940's most of it is column stilled.
Goslings Black Seal—a rich dark rum from Bermuda that was used to make the classic "Dark and Stormy" cocktail (Goslings, lime, and ginger beer).
Wray and Nephew—bartenders' overproof rum of choice, from Jamaica.

Shaking A cocktail-making technique for thick ingredients that need thorough mixing or chilling, which involves combining ingredients together in a cocktail shaker (often with ice).

Sloe gin A deep red/purple liqueur made from gin flavored with sugar and sloes.

Spear/flag A type of garnish. A piece of fruit cut into an arrowhead and attached to a toothpick/cocktail stick or the side of the glass.

Stirring A cocktail-making technique for clear drinks, which involves simply mixing the ingredients together in a mixing glass using a barspoon.

Sugar syrup Also known as simple syrup, gomme syrup, and sirop de gomme, this non-alcoholic syrup made from sugar is available commercially or can be made at home (see page 10). Often these syrups are flavored with fresh ingredients like mint and strawberry. This is done by simply adding the fruit or herb to the mixture of sugar and water when making the syrup.

Swizzling Refers to the act of vigorously stirring a drink, usually to encourage the frosting of the outside of the glass as well as to mix its ingredients. To swizzle, place a barspoon between your palms and move them quickly back and forth. Early swizzlers used a twig from a tree native to the Caribbean called the "swizzle stick tree".

Tequila A Mexican spirit, distilled from the juice of the blue agave plant, one of 400 species of agave, and produced only in certain regions of Mexico. There are four varieties: silver, gold, rested (reposado), and aged.

Tiki A Polynesian/Maori term (based on ornate wooden carvings that symbolized the first human man) used nowadays to define the popular drinks movement that originated on the West coast of America in the 1930s. Typically the drinks were rum heavy and served in ceramic Tiki mugs adorned with tropical fruit and flowers.

Triple sec A colorless orange-flavored liqueur similar to Cointreau.

Vermouth A fortified wine made in both Italy and France, flavored with herbs, sugar, and caramel and available in sweet, dry, red, and white versions. Kina Lillet (now known simply as Lillet) and Noilly Prat are highly regarded French vermouths. Cinzano and Martini & Rossi are well-known Italian brands.

Vodka Traditionally perceived as a colorless, tasteless, and odorless grain spirit in the West, vodka is also available flavored. Popular flavorings include bison grass (Zubrowka), blackcurrant, honey, lemon, lime, mandarin, melon, orange peel, pepper, and raspberry. Vodka produced in eastern Europe generally yields more flavorsome results.

Whiskey (American/Irish) or whisky (Scotch/Canadian) A spirit distilled from grain, malt, sugar, and yeast, first made in Scotland and Ireland more than 500 years ago. The various Scotch, Irish, Canadian, and American whiskies are very different. Scotch whisky is either a single malt or a blend of malt and grain whiskies—mixtures of the same whisky from different years or of different types of whiskies. Irish whiskey is made with a mixture of malted and unmalted barleys and is less pungent than Scotch because the barley is dried in a different type of kiln. All Canadian whisky is blended rye whisky, of a uniform high quality and rather light in both color, and taste. Originally only from Bourbon County, Kentucky, Bourbon whiskey is made from at least 51 percent corn and a blend of barley and rye or wheat, while American rye whiskey is made with at least 51 percent rye. Jack Daniel's is a "sour mash" whiskey produced at the Jack Daniel's distillery in Lynchburg, Tennessee.

Wine Where white or red wine is called for in a recipe, often the style of grape is mentioned by name. If not, it's time for you to experiment yourself!

Zest A thin slice of skin from the lemon, lime, or orange.

Index

Credits

Recipe Credits

All recipes by Ben Reed unless stated below:

Ghillie Basan, Gingery Chicken Tikka Kabobs with Minted Yogurt, Spicy Beef and Coconut Kofta Kabobs;
Jules Beresford, Marinated Olives; **Ross Dobson**, Spicy Cajun Mixed Nuts, Polenta Fries with Green Tabasco Mayonnaise, Phyllo Cigars with Halloumi; **Lydia France**, Crab Toasts with Chive, Caper, and Radish Salsa, Twice-marinated Salt Lime Chicken, Warm Spice-rubbed Potatoes with Rosemary Mayonnaise

Photography Credits

All photography by William Lingwood unless stated below:

Key: a=above, b=below, r=right, l=left, c=centre.

Caroline Arber © Cico Books, page 79 both; **Jan Baldwin**, pages 29c, 40l; **Henry Bourne**, page 51r; **Martin Brigdale**, pages 20l, 40r, 52l, 85r; **David Brittain**, pages 9c, 13l, 24r, 54r; **Simon Brown** © Cico Books, pages 10l, 69l, 101r; **Christopher Drake**, pages 30l, 34l, 68l; **Sandra Lane**, page 80r; **Tom Leighton**, pages 30r, 33 both; **Paul Massey**, pages 16r, 101l; **James Merrell**, page 86l; **Gloria Nicol** © Cico Books, page 76l; **Debi Patterson** © Cico Books, page 19l; **Claire Richardson**, page 43l; **Paul Ryan**, page 72l; **Mark Scott** © Cico Books, pages 57 both, 62r, 73l; **Chris Tubbs**, pages 51l, 55l, 76r; **Debi Treloar**, pages 5al, 5ar, 5bl, 10r, 14l (www.castlesinthesand.com), 15l, 16l, 20r, 24l, 27 both, 34r, 37c, 47c, 48r (www.powder-blue.co.uk), 59 both, 60r (www.chambredamis.com), 65 both , 66r, 71l (www.castlesinthesand.com), 75c, 80l, 80c, 85l, 86r, 89c, 90 both, 97l, 98 all, 101c; **Pia Tryde**, pages 52r, 62l, 103l; **Andrew Wood**, pages 83l, 94r (www.menagerhug.com/architect:www.m-a.fr); **Polly Wreford**, pages 13r, 19r, 37l; **Edina van der Wyck** © Cico Books, pages 42l, 61l, 93l